Foreword

When I wrote *The Internal Fungus Among Us,* I never imagined how many people would see themselves in those pages, searching for answers, craving energy, and longing to feel at home in their own bodies again. What began as my story became a shared story of healing, faith, and a return to balance.

But healing doesn't end when the symptoms fade or the tests come back clear. True healing asks for rhythm, for quiet moments that remind us we're still growing, still being renewed, still learning how to listen.

That's why I created *Soil to Soul.* It's not a checklist or a program. It's a practice, a sacred pause to breathe, reflect, and reconnect. These 90 days are meant to help you live what you've learned, to move from information into embodiment, from striving into flow.

Each page invites you to bring your whole self: your faith, your questions, your weariness, your wonder. Some days you'll write freely; other days you'll simply sit in stillness. Both are healing. Both count.

May this journal be a companion to your continued journey, a place to return to when life feels noisy, and a reminder that your body, mind, and spirit already know the way back to peace.

Keep listening. Keep growing. Keep returning to flow.

— Jackie

Preface

Rooted in Scripture and designed to support faith-centered healing of the mind, body, and spirit.

Healing asks something simple of us: presence.

Not perfection, not performance, just the willingness to slow down long enough to notice what's asking for care.

If you're holding this journal, chances are you've already begun that work. You've started listening to your body, paying attention to your thoughts, and learning what peace feels like. Now it's time to keep going—not with force, but with flow.

From Soil to Soul: Rooted & Renewed was created as a gentle rhythm of renewal.

Each day welcomes you to pause, breathe, reflect, and reconnect—physically, emotionally, and spiritually. Over the next ninety days, you'll witness small shifts that, like seeds, grow quietly beneath the surface.

Don't rush it. Healing unfolds in divine timing.

Some days will feel light, others heavy. Both are holy. What matters most is that you keep showing up with honesty, humility, and hope.

My prayer is that these pages help you find rest in the process, trust in your intuition, and gratitude for how beautifully your body and spirit were created to heal.

Here's to a season of flow in prayer, renewal, and reflection.

— Jackie

For my mom, whose love, strength, and quiet faith shaped the woman I became.

Her faith was lived through service—

    an altar server, choir singer, Eucharistic minister,

    and a devoted member of the Ladies of Saint Anne,

    the Daughters of Isabella,

    and the American Legion Ladies Auxiliary.

She made her Cursillo, feeding hearts and bellies

at the Bread of Life Soup Kitchen,

and gave her time wherever love was needed most.

She was the one who first taught me faith.

Forever loved, forever remembered.

"Healing isn't a destination.

It's a flow you return to,

one breath, one reflection, one prayer at a time."

— Jackie

"He makes everything beautiful in its time."

— Ecclesiastes 3:11 (NIV)

Acknowledgments

Much gratitude to everyone who has walked alongside me on this healing journey. Your support was the soil in which my work thrived and grew.

Thank you—

To the friends, readers, and mentors who shared their stories and life experiences. You reminded me that healing is possible.

To my family, my tribe, for reminding me of what it feels like to come back to myself. You are loving, funny, patient, and grounding in all the ways that matter most.

To the teachers, practitioners, faith organizations, and study groups who continue to inspire and motivate my work, for planting seeds of wisdom that keep growing long after the conversation ends.

To Andrea Baugher, Editor.

To Veronica St. Cyr, Design.

And most importantly, to God—the ultimate healer, teacher, and restorer of peace.

Every page is an offering of gratitude for the quiet miracles that happen when we finally slow down and listen.

How to Use This Journal

Healing is endless. You go back to this pattern one breath, one thought, and one prayer at a time. Longing for a certain flow, a feeling where you know you have arrived.

Every day is an invitation to slow down, listen to yourself, and see how faith and healing are connected in the simplest things. This 90-day journal was created to help you get back in touch with that rhythm.

Here's how to get started:

1. Make a sacred space.

Pick a time and place that is quiet, like the morning or evening, and sit still for 10 minutes. Bring your Bible, a pen, and an open mind.

2. Take your time reading the Scriptures.

Let the verse talk to you. Circle the words that stand out. Say them quietly. If they bring serenity, write them again.

3. Reflect with intention.

Use the guided prompts to think about what the passage says about your own healing on all levels: physical, emotional, and spiritual.

4. Write whatever comes to mind.

There is no "right" or "wrong" way to journal. Some days you'll write whole pages, and other days just one word. Both are sacred and valuable.

5. Finish with gratitude or prayer.

Let your last thought be one of letting go. Thank God, your body, or the process for what it's teaching you.

This journal is arranged in three parts, each leading you through 30 days of unique healing focus:

Days 1–30: Root to Rise

"They will be like a tree planted by streams of water, which yields its fruit in season and whose leaf does not wither—whatever they do prospers."
— Psalm 1:3 (NIV)

Healing begins beneath the surface. This first part is about slowing down, breathing deeply, and grounding yourself in faith before growth begins.

Days 31–60: Rest and Restore

"Come to me, all you who are weary and burdened, and I will give you rest."
— Matthew 11:28 (NIV)

Stillness makes healing deeper. For the next 30 days, you'll let go of everything you've been carrying and allow reflection to be a way to heal.

Days 61–90: Renew and Flourish

"See, I am doing a new thing! Now it springs up; do you not perceive it?"
— Isaiah 43:19 (NIV)

This last part is about renewal, building on what's already there, and celebrating how far you've come. Grow in faith, peace, and wholeness.

After 90 days, these short breaks turn into something deeper: a rhythm of regeneration that strengthens your body and grounds your spirit.

Begin where you are. Let the pages hold you close, and remember that you are not alone. And believe that every thought, like every seed, has the power to grow into lasting healing.

Let's begin.

 Part 1: Root to Rise *(Days 1–30)*

> "They will be like a tree planted by streams of water, which yields its fruit in season and whose leaf does not wither—whatever they do prospers."
>
> *— Psalm 1:3 (NIV)*

Every healing starts beneath the surface.

This first part of your journey invites grounding, faith, and reconnection to your inner wisdom.

Here, you'll learn to take things slowly, really listen, and have faith in the growth process that starts unseen.

Every day is a seed.

Every reflection, a root reaching deeper toward renewal.

* * *

Day 1: Begin in the Body

Scripture:

"Do you not know that your bodies are temples of the Holy Spirit, who is in you...?"

— 1 Corinthians 6:19 (NIV)

* * *

Affirmation:

I am learning to trust my body as a messenger of healing.

Reflection Prompt:

What does your body need more of today: rest, nourishment, gentleness?

Journal Space:

Reflect & Respond

[1]

---

[1] Consider sipping a warm cup of chamomile or herbal tea.

Day 2: Healing From the Root

Scripture:

"He heals the brokenhearted and saves those who are crushed in spirit."

— Psalm 34:18 (NIV)

* * *

Affirmation:

I am open to healing at the deepest level—physically, emotionally, and spiritually.

Reflection Prompt:

What "root cause" is your body revealing beneath your current symptoms or stress?

Journal Space:

Reflect & Respond

[2]

---

2 Try taking a ten-minute walk outdoors.

Day 3: The Peace Response

Scripture:

"Peace I leave with you; my peace I give you. I do not give to you as the world gives."

— John 14:27 (NIV)

* * *

Affirmation:

I am safe to exhale and to allow peace to regulate my body.

Reflection Prompt:

How does your body respond when you shift from fight-or-flight into peace?

Journal Space:

Reflect & Respond

[3]

---

[3] Stretch your arms toward the sky, hold them there, and breathe deeply.

Day 4: Cleansing and Renewal

Scripture:

"Create in me a pure heart, O God, and renew a steadfast spirit within me."

— *Psalm 51:10 (NIV)*

* * *

Affirmation:

I am gently releasing what no longer serves my healing process.

Reflection Prompt:

What toxins, physical or emotional, might your body be ready to let go of?

Journal Space:

Reflect & Respond

4

---

[4] Consider drinking a full glass of water thirty minutes before your next meal.

Day 5: Nourished by Light

Scripture:

"The eye is the lamp of the body. If your eyes are healthy, your whole body will be full of light."

— *Matthew 6:22 (NIV)*

* * *

Affirmation:

I am nourished by light, truth, and clarity in every cell of my body.

Reflection Prompt:

What brings light into your body and life? How can you create more of it today?

Journal Space:

Reflect & Respond

[5]

---

[5] Find a comfortable place to sit outside and let the sunlight hit your face for twenty minutes.

Day 6: The Wisdom Within

Scripture:

"I praise you because I am fearfully and wonderfully made; your works are wonderful, I know that full well."

— *Psalm 139:14 (NIV)*

* * *

Affirmation:

I am wonderfully made; my body holds the wisdom to heal itself.

Reflection Prompt:

Where do you need to trust your body's intelligence today?

Journal Space:

Reflect & Respond

[6]

---

[6] Take five slow, intentional breaths before you start your day.

Day 7: Rest as Medicine

Scripture:

"Come to me, all you who are weary and burdened, and I will give you rest."

— *Matthew 11:28 (NIV)*

* * *

Affirmation:

I am allowed to rest; rest is an *active* part of my healing.

Reflection Prompt:

What happens in your body and mind when you allow yourself to rest without guilt?

Journal Space:

Reflect & Respond

7

---

[7] Make a nourishing breakfast (or first meal of the day) with one fresh ingredient.

Week 1 Reflection: Root Awareness

Scripture:

"Stand firm, and you will win life."

— *Luke 21:19 (NIV)*

* * *

Affirmation:

I am learning to be grounded in serenity, awareness, and presence.

Reflection Prompts:

Think about your first week for a few quiet minutes. You have been reconnecting with your body, your breath, and your core for the past few days.

Reflect on what has changed, even if it's just a little bit or below the surface.

1. Which moments or verses felt most healing this week?
2. Where in your body do you feel more grounded or at ease?
3. What old thought or habit began to loosen its hold?
4. How can you create more space for rest and nourishment in the week ahead?

Reflect & Respond

Day 8: Release What's Heavy

Scripture:

"Cast all your anxiety on him because he cares for you."

— *1 Peter 5:7 (NIV)*

* * *

Affirmation:

I am releasing what's heavy and making space to be carried.

Reflection Prompt:

What burdens or beliefs might your body be ready to release?

Journal Space:

Reflect & Respond

[8]

---

[8] Explore how it feels to sit in silence for two minutes and listen to your heartbeat.

Day 9: Breath of Renewal

Scripture:

"The Spirit of God has made me; the breath of the Almighty gives me life."

— Job 33:4 (NIV)

* * *

Affirmation:

I am renewed with each breath; life flows freely through me.

Reflection Prompt:

How does your breath change when you focus on feeling safe and supported?

Journal Space:

Reflect & Respond

9

---

[9] Write down three things your body has done well for you today.

Day 10: Strength in Stillness

Scripture:

"The Lord will fight for you; you need only to be still." — *Exodus 14:14 (NIV)*

* * *

Affirmation:

I am strengthened in stillness; my body heals in the calm.

Reflection Prompt:

How might stillness become your daily medicine?

Journal Space:

Reflect & Respond

10

---

[10] Take a warm bath or shower and let the water calm your nervous system.

Day 11: Listening Beneath the Noise

Scripture:

"The Lord will guide you always; he will satisfy your needs in a sun-scorched land and will strengthen your frame."

— *Isaiah 58:11 (NIV)*

* * *

Affirmation:

I am tuning out the noise so I can hear what my body truly needs.

Reflection Prompt:

What external noise or inner chatter keeps you from noticing what your body is asking for?

Journal Space:

Reflect & Respond

---

[11] Consider turning your phone on silent for one hour and resting.

Day 12: The Gift of Movement

Scripture:

"'In him we live and move and have our being.' As some of your own poets have said, 'We are his offspring.'"

— *Acts 17:28 (NIV)*

* * *

Affirmation:

I love how my body moves and shows me what life is all about.

Reflection Prompt:

How can today's movement be an act of gratitude instead of duty?

Journal Space:

Reflect & Respond

[12]

---

[12] Consider replacing one sugary drink with water and a lemon wedge today.

Day 13: Gentle Detox

Scripture:

"Let us purify ourselves from everything that contaminates body and spirit, perfecting holiness out of reverence for God."

— *2 Corinthians 7:1 (NIV)*

* * *

Affirmation:

I am clearing space for renewal in both body and mind.

Reflection Prompt:

What simple practice allows you to detoxify, physically or mentally, without using force?

Journal Space:

Reflect & Respond

13

---

[13] Before each meal, try one gentle neck stretch while having a positive thought.

Day 14: Rooted in Truth

Scripture:

"Then you will know the truth, and the truth will set you free."

— *John 8:32 (NIV)*

* * *

Affirmation:

I am grounded in truth, which provides me freedom in both mind and body.

Reflection Prompt:

What truth about your health or healing are you willing to embrace, even if it is uncomfortable?

Journal Space:

Reflect & Respond

[14]

Week 2 Reflection: Body Awareness

Scripture:

"Be still, and know that I am God."

— *Psalm 46:10 (NIV)*

* * *

Affirmation:

I am learning to pause and listen to my body with compassion.

Reflection Prompts:

This week asked you to pay closer attention to how your body speaks to you.

Through stillness and movement, you practiced noticing ease, tension, and the quiet wisdom held within your physical experience.

1. What messages is your body telling you this week?
2. Where in your body did you feel the most at ease or stressed out?
3. How did stillness or movement help you heal?
4. What will you carry over to the following week?

Reflect & Respond

Day 15: Hydration and Healing

Scripture:

"Whoever believes in me, as Scripture has said, rivers of living water will flow from within them."

—*John 7:38 (NIV)*

* * *

Affirmation:

Life flows easily through me; I am well-hydrated both physically and spiritually.

Reflection Prompt:

Where in your life are you ready to allow more flow or emotional release?

Journal Space:

Reflect & Respond

[15]

---

[15] Notice five things you can see around your home, and then express gratitude.

Day 16: The Power of Rest

Scripture:

"In peace I will lie down and sleep, for you alone, Lord, make me dwell in safety."

— *Psalm 4:8 (NIV)*

* * *

Affirmation:

I embrace rest as a holy reset.

Reflection Prompt:

What prevents you from getting enough sleep, and how can you honor your need for it tonight?

Journal Space:

Reflect & Respond

[16]

---

[16] Remember to smell the richness in your dinner; consider praying before tasting.

Day 17: Clearing the Mind

Scripture:

"Do not conform to the pattern of this world, but be transformed by the renewing of your mind."

— *Romans 12:2 (NIV)*

* * *

Affirmation:

I am clearing mental clutter and making space for peace.

Reflection Prompt:

What thought pattern are you ready to release so your mind can reset?

Journal Space:

Reflect & Respond

---

[17] Try tasting a piece of fresh fruit mindfully.

Day 18: Digesting Life

Scripture:

"Pleasant words are a honeycomb, sweet to the soul and healing to the bones."

— *Proverbs 16:24 (NIV)*

* * *

Affirmation:

I'm learning how to speak kindly to and about myself.

Reflection Prompt:

What mental or emotional "food" have you been consuming that nourishes or drains you?

Journal Space:

Reflect & Respond

[18]

---

[18] Try relaxing your jaw and lowering your shoulders.

Day 19: Energy in Alignment

Scripture:

"God is our refuge and strength, an ever-present help in trouble."

— Psalm 46:1 (NIV)

* * *

Affirmation:

I am fueled by joy, which flows through my heart and soul.

Reflection Prompt:

Where are you pouring energy that isn't helping you heal?

Journal Space:

Reflect & Respond

---

[19] Treat yourself by going to bed fifteen minutes earlier than usual, if it's available to you.

Day 20: Gratitude as Grounding

Scripture:

"Give thanks in all circumstances; for this is God's will for you in Christ Jesus."

— *1 Thessalonians 5:18 (NIV)*

* * *

Affirmation:

I am anchored in gratitude that centers my soul.

Reflection Prompt:

List three things your body has done for you this week that deserve thanks.

Journal Space:

Reflect & Respond

---

[20] Try deep belly breathing for one minute, with gratitude for each breath.

Day 21: Boundaries and Balance

Scripture:

"Let your 'Yes' be yes, and your 'No,' no."

— *Matthew 5:37 (NIV)*

* * *

Affirmation:

Today I am free to set healthy boundaries that protect my peace and energy.

Reflection Prompt:

How might saying "no" allow for more healing and balance?

Journal Space:

Reflect & Respond

21

---

[21] Try a quick cleanup of one small space to help clear your mind.

Week 3 Reflection: Mind and Body Harmony

Scripture:

"You will keep in perfect peace those whose minds are steadfast, because they trust in you."

— Isaiah 26:3 (NIV)

* * *

Affirmation:

I am learning to align my mind and body in peace and purpose.

Reflection Prompts:

This week focused on the relationship between your thoughts and how you feel.

You explored how peace, trust, and awareness can bring your mind and body back into alignment.

1. How have your thoughts affected how you feel this week?
2. What beliefs or anxieties are you willing to let go of so your healing can continue?
3. Which practices this week naturally balanced your body and spirit?
4. How can you incorporate more peace into your everyday activities moving forward?

Reflect & Respond

Day 22: Rooted in Faith, Not Fear

Scripture:

"When I am afraid, I put my trust in you."

— *Psalm 56:3 (NIV)*

* * *

Affirmation:

I am grounded in faith, which soothes my nervous system and renews my body.

Reflection Prompt:

What does faith feel like in your body compared to fear?

Journal Space:

Reflect & Respond

[22]

---

[22] Consider looking in the mirror and saying one kind thing to yourself.

Day 23: Healing Through Connection

Scripture:

"Carry each other's burdens, and in this way you will fulfill the law of Christ."

— *Galatians 6:2 (NIV)*

* * *

Affirmation:

I am open to connection; healing happens in relationship, not isolation.

Reflection Prompt:

Who helps you feel seen, supported, or safe on your healing journey?

Journal Space:

Reflect & Respond

[23]

---

[23] Consider taking a screen/digital break for thirty minutes.

Day 24: Letting Go of What No Longer Serves

Scripture:

"Forget the former things; do not dwell on the past."

— *Isaiah 43:18 (NIV)*

* * *

Affirmation:

I am shedding behaviors, thoughts, and attachments that are impeding my healing.

Reflection Prompt:

What are you willing to let go of to make way for fresh growth?

Journal Space:

Reflect & Respond

[24]

---

24 Fill a 30-ounce water bottle and keep sipping all morning.

Day 25: The Soil of Surrender

Scripture:

"Be still before the Lord and wait patiently for him."

— *Psalm 37:7 (NIV)*

* * *

Affirmation:

I am surrendering the outcome and trusting in divine timing.

Reflection Prompt:

Which part of your healing are you trying to control instead of giving it over?

Journal Space:

Reflect & Respond

25

---

[25] Close your eyes and spend five minutes visualizing peace filling your whole body.

Day 26: Listening With Love

Scripture:

"Everyone should be quick to listen, slow to speak, and slow to become angry."

—*James 1:19 (NIV)*

* * *

Affirmation:

I am lovingly listening to my body, to my emotions, and to others.

Reflection Prompt:

What messages could your body or heart be sending under the noise?

Journal Space:

Reflect & Respond

[26]

---

[26] When you pray, try lighting a beeswax candle or diffusing essential oils to help calm your senses.

Day 27: The Gift of Simplicity

Scripture:

"But godliness with contentment is great gain."

— *1 Timothy 6:6 (NIV)*

* * *

Affirmation:

I'm returning to simplicity; what's necessary is enough.

Reflection Prompt:

Could simplifying your environment or schedule help you heal?

Journal Space:

Reflect & Respond

27

---

[27] Practice sitting up straight, feeling your strength, for the next
ten breaths.

Day 28: Grounded Gratitude

Scripture:

"Rooted and built up in him, strengthened in the faith as you were taught, and overflowing with thankfulness."

— *Colossians 2:7 (NIV)*

* * *

Affirmation:

I am grounded in appreciation, which strengthens my spirit.

Reflection Prompt:

How does appreciation affect your energy and outlook today?

Journal Space:

Reflect & Respond

---

[28] Consider a gentle spine stretch or wrist rotation.

Week 4 Reflection: Rooted Renewal

Scripture:

"He refreshes my soul. He guides me along the right paths for his name's sake."

— *Psalm 23:3 (NIV)*

* * *

Affirmation:

I am renewing myself physically, mentally, and spiritually.

Reflection Prompts:

This week allowed you to notice renewal happening quietly, without force.

You may have sensed small shifts in energy, clarity, or faith that signal growth taking place beneath the surface.

1. What changes or breakthroughs have begun to surface in your healing?
2. Where have you seen renewal happening quietly beneath the surface?
3. Which relationships, practices, or routines have supported your restoration?
4. As you enter the next phase, what does renewal mean to you right now?

Reflect & Respond

Day 29: Resilience Rising

Scripture:

"They will be like a tree planted by the water that sends out its roots by the stream."

— Jeremiah 17:8 (NIV)

* * *

Affirmation:

I am steadily growing through every obstacle, rooted in strength.

Reflection Prompt:

What experience felt like it was breaking you, but it actually helped you become yourself?

Journal Space:

Reflect & Respond

[29]

---

[29] Explore journaling your current emotions without judgment.

Day 30: Whole and Rooted

Scripture:

"The Lord will strengthen you and protect you from the evil one."

— *2 Thessalonians 3:3 (NIV)*

* * *

Affirmation:

I am rooted, faith centered, and ready to rise.

Reflection Prompt:

Looking back over the past thirty days, what new roots have been established in your healing?

Journal Space:

Reflect & Respond

---

[30] Try to take a slow walk, in prayer, after a meal.

Pause & Pray

❁ Part 2: Rest & Restore *(Days 31–60)*

"He makes me lie down in green pastures,

he leads me beside quiet waters,

he refreshes my soul."

— Psalm 23:2–3 (NIV)

Healing does not always require action.

Sometimes it begins in quietness, in the silent surrender that allows your body and mind to finally breathe.

This section of this journey is about rest as medicine, serenity as power, and gentleness as strength.

Allow your nervous system to restore itself.

Allow forgiveness to soften you.

Allow calmness to become your new rhythm.

You are free to rest.

You can heal safely.

* * *

Day 31: Permission to Rest

Scripture:

"In repentance and rest is your salvation, in quietness and trust is your strength."

— *Isaiah 30:15 (NIV)*

* * *

Affirmation:

I am allowed to rest deeply without guilt or resistance.

Reflection Prompt:

How can you honor your body's need for rest today without explaining or justifying it?

Journal Space:

Reflect & Respond

31

---

[31] Consider doing one small act of kindness for a friend or a stranger.

Day 32: Nervous System Peace

Scripture:

"The Lord gives strength to his people; the Lord blesses his people with peace."

— *Psalm 29:11 (NIV)*

* * *

Affirmation:

I am inviting my body to feel calm, safe, and peaceful.

Reflection Prompt:

What helps your body transition smoothly from stress to relaxation?

Journal Page:

Reflect & Respond

³²

---

³² Try putting on a calming video for a deep, gentle relaxation.

Day 33: Release and Restore

Scripture:

"He gives strength to the weary and increases the power of the weak."

— Isaiah 40:29 (NIV)

* * *

Affirmation:

I am releasing the weight of what I cannot carry and choosing rest instead.

Reflection Prompt:

What would it look like to let strength rise in you today instead of strain?

Journal Space:

Reflect & Respond

[33]

---

[33] Place your hand over your heart, feel how special you are, and breathe deeply.

Day 34: The Healing Break

Scripture:

"He makes me lie down in green pastures, he leads me beside quiet waters."

— *Psalm 23:2 (NIV)*

* * *

Affirmation:

I'm learning to slow down before pushing and relax before reaching.

Reflection Prompt:

Where in your day could you take a break and breathe instead of pushing through?

Journal Space:

Reflect & Respond

---

[34] Listen to something uplifting while you get ready today, and maybe dance too.

Day 35: Forgiveness as Medicine

Scripture:

"Bear with each other and forgive one another if any of you has a grievance."

— *Colossians 3:13 (NIV)*

* * *

Affirmation:

I am freeing my body and heart through forgiveness.

Reflection Prompt:

Is there someone, including yourself, you can forgive to create space for healing?

Journal Space:

Reflect & Respond

35

---

[35] Try saying no to something that drains you.

Week 5 Reflection Rest in Grace

Scripture:

"My presence will go with you, and I will give you rest."

— *Exodus 33:14 (NIV)*

* * *

Affirmation:

I'm learning to rest in divine presence and tranquility.

Reflection Prompts:

This week invited you to soften your effort and rest more fully.

By allowing grace instead of striving, you gave your body and spirit space to restore naturally.

1. How did your body respond to greater rest this week?
2. What times in solitude provided you the most clarity?
3. What did you notice when you stopped striving and simply allowed?
4. How will you continue to treat your rest as something precious in the coming week?

Reflect & Respond

Day 36: Grace in the Gaps

Scripture:

"My grace is sufficient for you, for My power is made perfect in weakness."

— 2 Corinthians 12:9

Affirmation:

I release perfection and receive grace. Even in the gaps, I am held, guided, and growing.

Reflection Prompt:

Sometimes healing doesn't move in neat lines or perfect order. Sometimes there are pauses, missed steps, or moments we didn't plan for—and still, growth happens.

Where in your life are you being invited to soften your grip on "getting it right" and trust that grace is already at work?

Journal Space:

Reflect & Respond

---

[36] If you missed a day, a step, or a promise you made to yourself, don't rush to make up for it. Instead, take one slow breath and begin again.

Day 37: Rhythm of Renewal

Scripture:

"Cast all your anxiety on him because he cares for you."

— *1 Peter 5:7 (NIV)*

* * *

Affirmation:

I am surrendering stress and allowing peace to wash over me.

Reflection Prompt:

What helps you remember that you don't have to carry it all alone?

Journal Space:

Reflect & Respond

[37]

---

[37] Reflect on a time He was there for you and you didn't have to do it alone.

Day 38: Softening the Edges

Scripture:

"Let your gentleness be evident to all. The Lord is near."

— *Philippians 4:5 (NIV)*

* * *

Affirmation:

I am learning to meet myself with gentleness always and forever.

Reflection Prompt:

What would it be like to soften the way you talk to or care for yourself today?

Journal Space:

Reflect & Respond

---

[38] Try putting a cosmetic mirror in your pocket. Throughout the day, reflect and say, "I am more than enough."

Day 39: Healing Sleep

Scripture:

"When you lie down, you will not be afraid; when you lie down, your sleep will be sweet."

— *Proverbs 3:24 (NIV)*

* * *

Affirmation:

I am allowing my body to heal, restore, and regenerate through deep sleep.

Reflection Prompt:

How can you prepare your body and mind tonight for peaceful, restorative sleep?

Journal Space:

Reflect & Respond

[39]

---

[39] Try taking a simple leg stretch break.

Day 40: Peace in the Present

Scripture:

"Do not worry about tomorrow, for tomorrow will worry about itself."

— *Matthew 6:34 (NIV)*

* * *

Affirmation:

I am present in this moment; peace lives within.

Reflection Prompt:

How can being totally present in the moment affect how your body feels?

Journal Space:

Reflect & Respond

40

---

[40] Put your bare feet on the ground for a moment and feel the earth.

Day 41: Breathe Again

Scripture:

"The Spirit of God has made me; the breath of the Almighty gives me life."

— Job 33:4

* * *

Affirmation:

I am reconnecting with the breath that restores my peace.

Reflection Prompt:

How does deep breathing change the way your body feels in this moment?

Journal Space:

Reflect & Respond

41

---

[41] Breathe in as you count to four, hold for two, then breathe out for seven.

Day 42: Healing Through Stillness

Scripture:

"The Lord will fight for you; you need only to be still."

— *Exodus 14:14 (NIV)*

* * *

Affirmation:

I am discovering wisdom in the quiet.

Reflection Prompt:

Where do you feel reluctant to slow down, and what would happen if you did?

Journal Space:

Reflect & Respond

[42]

---

⁴² Sit near a window and watch the sky in stillness.

Week 6 Reflection: Gentle Restoration

Scripture:

"He heals the brokenhearted and binds up their wounds."

— *Psalm 147:3 (NIV)*

* * *

Affirmation:

I am discovering that gentleness heals what force cannot.

Reflection Prompts:

This week emphasized gentleness as a healing force.

You practiced compassion toward yourself and discovered how softness can reach places that force never could.

1. How has rest helped you understand your body's genuine needs?
2. How have you shown yourself compassion this week?
3. What moments of happiness or peace surprised you?
4. How might you continue letting gentleness lead your healing?

Reflect & Respond

Day 43: The Gift of Silence

Scripture:

"The Lord is in his holy temple; let all the earth be silent before him."

— *Habakkuk 2:20 (NIV)*

* * *

Affirmation:

I am comfortable with solitude; that is where healing begins.

Reflection Prompt:

What might silence reveal to you that constant noise cannot?

Journal Space:

Reflect & Respond

---

[43] Give yourself the gift of silence by taking a walk in the woods or sitting beside a tree in the yard.

Day 44: Letting Light In

Scripture:

"For you were once darkness, but now you are light in the Lord. Live as children of light."

— *Ephesians 5:8 (NIV)*

* * *

Affirmation:

I am allowing light and truth to flood every area of my being that was before hidden in shadow.

Reflection Prompt:

What "light" has come into your life since you started this journey?

Journal Space:

Reflect & Respond

[44]

---

[44] Light a candle tonight and think about why you are shining more brightly.

Day 45: Body of Compassion

Scripture:

"As God's chosen people, clothe yourselves with compassion, kindness, humility, gentleness, and patience."

— *Colossians 3:12 (NIV)*

* * *

Affirmation:

I treat my body with the same compassion that I would show a loved one.

Reflection Prompt:

Where could you soften your self-talk or expectations to allow deeper healing?

Journal Space:

Reflect & Respond

[45]

---

[45] Replace negative self-talk with one encouraging affirmation.

Day 46: Joy as Medicine

Scripture:

"A cheerful heart is good medicine, but a crushed spirit dries up the bones."

— *Proverbs 17:22 (NIV)*

* * *

Affirmation:

I allow joy to flow freely through my body.

Reflection Prompt:

What tiny joys could you enjoy today as part of your recovery journey?

Journal Space:

Reflect & Respond

[46]

---

[46] Step outside and breathe in the fresh air three times today.

Day 47: Let It Be Easy

Scripture:

"My yoke is easy, and my burden is light."

— *Matthew 11:30 (NIV)*

* * *

Affirmation:

I am allowed to let healing be easy and steady.

Reflection Prompt:

What would change if you trusted that healing doesn't have to be hard?

Journal Space:

Reflect & Respond

[47]

---

[47] Try a gentle self-massage on your temples. You matter.

Day 48: Peaceful Boundaries

Scripture:

"Let the peace of Christ rule in your hearts."

— *Colossians 3:15 (NIV)*

* * *

Affirmation:

I am protecting my peace as an act of devotion.

Reflection Prompt:

What energy could you conserve, or what emotional or physical boundaries could you strengthen to protect your peace?

Journal Space:

Reflect & Respond

---

[48] Give yourself a fifteen-minute pause, just for you.

Day 49: Wholeness in Waiting

Scripture:

"The Lord is good to those whose hope is in him, to the one who seeks him."

— *Lamentations 3:25 (NIV)*

* * *

Affirmation:

I am hopeful even as I wait for full healing to take place.

Reflection Prompt:

What if this waiting period is actually a vital part of your healing?

Journal Space:

Reflect & Respond

---

[49] Be hopeful in the waiting, and let yourself smile.

Week 7 Reflection: Peace in the Process

Scripture:

"You will go out in joy and be led forth in peace."

— *Isaiah 55:12 (NIV)*

* * *

Affirmation:

I am walking in peace, even while in the process.

Reflection Prompts:

This week reminded you that healing unfolds in its own timing.

As you released urgency and control, you may have noticed peace emerging simply by allowing the process to be what it is.

1. Which aspects of your life have softened since you started allowing rather than forcing?
2. How have rest and surrender impacted your perspective on healing?
3. Where have you witnessed small signs of renewal this week?
4. What do you hope to carry over into the next phase?

Reflect & Respond

Day 50: Mercy in Motion

Scripture:

"The Lord makes firm the steps of the one who delights in him."

— *Psalm 37:23 (NIV)*

* * *

Affirmation:

Mercy directs my steps with ease and alignment.

Reflection Prompt:

How does "moving with mercy " appear for you today?

Journal Space:

Reflect & Respond

[50]

---

[50] Consider inviting someone over for coffee.

Day 51: Trusting Divine Timing

Scripture:

"He has made everything beautiful in its time."

— *Ecclesiastes 3:11 (NIV)*

* * *

Affirmation:

I trust that healing will happen when it is meant to, not when I want it to.

Reflection Prompt:

Where might patience provide greater peace than control right now?

Journal Space:

Reflect & Respond

---

[51] Set a small, achievable goal for today.

Day 52: The Body Remembers

Scripture:

"The Lord is close to the brokenhearted and saves those who are crushed in spirit."

— *Psalm 34:18 (NIV)*

* * *

Affirmation:

I am allowing my body to release old pain and welcome comfort.

Reflection Prompt:

Which part of your body holds tension or memory, and what might it need to feel safe enough to let go?

Journal Space:

Reflect & Respond

---

52 Today, pray a scripture over your body and believe it is so.

Day 53: Restoring Rhythm

Scripture:

"There remains, then, a Sabbath-rest for the people of God."

— *Hebrews 4:9 (NIV)*

* * *

Affirmation:

I am honoring my natural rhythm of rest and renewal.

Reflection Prompt:

How could incorporating relaxation into your daily routine support your long-term healing?

Journal Space:

Reflect & Respond

---

[53] Allow rest without guilt for ten minutes, thirty minutes if you're feeling brave.

Day 54: Cleansing Emotions

Scripture:

"Wash me, and I will be whiter than snow."

— *Psalm 51:7 (NIV)*

* * *

Affirmation:

I am releasing stored emotions that no longer serve my well-being.

Reflection Prompt:

What emotion has been begging to be felt, expressed, or released?

Journal Space:

Reflect & Respond

54

---

[54] Allow time to journal how your body feels holding emotions that don't serve you.

Day 55: Letting Go of Resistance

Scripture:

"Be still before the Lord and wait patiently for him."

— *Psalm 37:7 (NIV)*

* * *

Affirmation:

I am letting stillness guide my healing with ease.

Reflection Prompt:

What does surrender look like for you today—in your body, your habits, or your heart?

Journal Space:

Reflect & Respond

[55]

---

[55] Try wearing cozy clothing that helps your body relax and just "be."

Day 56: Faith Over Frustration

Scripture:

"Do not be anxious about anything, but in every situation, by prayer and petition, with thanksgiving, present your requests to God."

— *Philippians 4:6 (NIV)*

* * *

Affirmation:

I choose faith over frustration, patience over panic.

Reflection Prompt:

How does your body respond when you choose faith instead of fear?

Journal Space:

Reflect & Respond

[56]

---

[56] Place one hand on your stomach, one on your heart, and practice calm breathing.

Week 8 Reflection: Seeds of Joy

Scripture:

"The joy of the Lord is your strength."

— *Nehemiah 8:10 (NIV)*

* * *

Affirmation:

I am creating joy that strengthens me from the inside out.

Reflection Prompts:

This week encouraged you to notice joy as nourishment.

Even small moments of gratitude or lightness may have strengthened your energy and supported continued healing.

1. Which simple moments have brought you joy or laughter this week?
2. How has thankfulness affected your energy and mood?
3. Where do you feel new growth emerging?
4. What intention will help you keep nurturing joy through the next week?

Reflect & Respond

Day 57: Healing Flow

Scripture:

"Whoever believes in me...rivers of living water will flow from within them."

— *John 7:38 (NIV)*

* * *

Affirmation:

I am in the flow of healing, and it passes through me with ease and compassion.

Reflection Prompt:

What helps you stay in the flow physically, emotionally, or spiritually?

Journal Space:

Reflect & Respond

[57]

---

[57] Consider sipping a warm drink without caffeine today.

Day 58: Peaceful Nutrition

Scripture:

"So whether you eat or drink or whatever you do, do it all for the glory of God."

— *1 Corinthians 10:31 (NIV)*

* * *

Affirmation:

I nourish my body with foods and thoughts that promote life.

Reflection Prompt:

How might eating or nurturing yourself become a form of gratitude today?

Journal Space:

Reflect & Respond

---

[58] Try nourishing yourself today by replacing a processed snack with a fresh one.

Day 59: Willing in Spirit

Scripture:

"Restore to me the joy of your salvation and grant me a willing spirit, to sustain me."

— *Psalm 51:12 (NIV)*

* * *

Affirmation:

I am restoring my health with a willing spirit and heart.

Reflection Prompt:

What gives you a sense of calm and a willing spirit to carry you through the healing process?

Journal Space:

Reflect & Respond

59

---

59 While sipping on water, thank God for hydration.

Day 60: Rested and Renewed

Scripture:

"My soul finds rest in God; my salvation comes from him."

— *Psalm 62:1 (NIV)*

* * *

Affirmation:

I am renewed in rest, restored in faith, and ready for growth.

Reflection Prompt:

How has rest changed your body, your thoughts, and your relationship to healing?

Journal Space:

Reflect & Respond

[60]

---

[60] Listen to a peaceful podcast or worship playlist while you rest.

Pause & Pray

 Part 3: Renew & Flourish *(Days 61–90)*

"See, I am doing a new thing! Now it springs up; do you not perceive it?"

— *Isaiah 43:19 (NIV)*

This final part of your journey welcomes renewal from the inside out—to rise with joy, strength, and thankfulness for how far you've come.

You've worked toward rooting deeply and resting completely.

It's now time to flourish by embodying the healing you've cultivated and living from that wholeness every day.

* * *

Day 61: A New Beginning

Scripture:

"See, I am doing a new thing! Now it springs up; do you not perceive it?"

— Isaiah 43:19 (NIV)

* * *

Affirmation:

I am stepping into new beginnings with strength, trust, and joy.

Reflection Prompt:

What fresh development or opportunity are you starting to notice in your life right now?

Journal Space:

Reflect & Respond

---

[61] Take a step toward peace by decluttering one tiny area (drawer, counter, purse).

Day 62: Rising Energy

Scripture:

"The Lord is my strength and my shield; my heart trusts in him, and he helps me."

— Psalm 28:7 (NIV)

* * *

Affirmation:

I am rising in joy, vitality, and purpose that flow from within.

Reflection Prompt:

When do you feel the most alive and strong in spirit?

Journal Space:

Reflect & Respond

---

[62] Take a break to count your blessings using your fingers (and toes if you feel inspired).

Day 63: Refreshed

Scripture:

"I will refresh the weary and satisfy the faint."

—*Jeremiah 31:25 (NIV)*

* * *

Affirmation:

I am lighthearted, free, and unburdened by what formerly weighed me down.

Reflection Prompt:

How can you choose lightness today as you talk with those around you?

Journal Space:

Reflect & Respond

63

---

[63] Try a simple prayer walk, or walking meditation, even just around your room.

Week 9 Reflection: Flourish in Faith

Scripture:

"The righteous will flourish like a palm tree, they will grow like a cedar of Lebanon."

— *Psalm 92:12 (NIV)*

* * *

Affirmation:

I am thriving in faith and rooted in peace.

Reflection Prompts:

This week focused on growth that feels rooted and steady.

You began to recognize confidence, trust, and faith taking shape in ways that feel natural and grounded.

1. Where have you seen new growth or confidence emerging?
2. How have you seen faith support your healing journey?
3. What blessings or opportunities have blossomed this week?
4. How can you keep nurturing your growth while staying grounded?

Reflect & Respond

Day 64: Bloom Where You Are

Scripture:

"They are planted in the house of the Lord; they will flourish in the courts of our God."

— Psalm 92:13 (NIV)

* * *

Affirmation:

I'm blossoming exactly where I've been planted.

Reflection Prompt:

What can you enjoy or cultivate in this season rather than waiting for the next?

Journal Space:

Reflect & Respond

[64]

---

[64] Get yourself flowers today, or re-pot a plant and play in the dirt.

Day 65: Overflowing Gratitude

Scripture:

"Give thanks to the Lord, for he is good; his love endures forever."

— *Psalm 107:1 (NIV)*

* * *

Affirmation:

I am filled with appreciation, which promotes healing and happiness.

Reflection Prompt:

What three things today fill your heart with genuine gratitude?

Journal Space:

Reflect & Respond

[65]

---

[65] Try releasing tension by smiling.

Day 66: Confidence in Healing

Scripture:

"The Lord is my strength and my defense; he has become my salvation."

— *Exodus 15:2 (NIV)*

* * *

Affirmation:

I am confident in my body's divine ability to heal and thrive.

Reflection Prompt:

What does confidence in your body's healing look or feel like today?

Journal Space:

Reflect & Respond

---

[66] Try a peppermint or lavender scent to calm your mind.

Day 67: Radiant Health

Scripture:

"A cheerful heart is good medicine…"

— *Proverbs 17:22 (NIV)*

* * *

Affirmation:

I am radiating health, wholeness, and peaceful energy.

Reflection Prompt:

What daily actions or thoughts help you shine from the inside out? And where could you fit this into a daily practice?

Journal Space:

Reflect & Respond

[67]

---

[67] Look for the goodness in others reflecting back at you.

Day 68: Wholeness Restored

Scripture:

"The Lord will restore you and make you strong, firm, and steadfast."

— 1 Peter 5:10 (NIV)

* * *

Affirmation:

I am whole and restored in strength, spirit, and peace.

Reflection Prompt:

Which part of you feels most "restored" right now, and how can you celebrate that progress?

Journal Space:

Reflect & Respond

[68]

---

[68] Give yourself permission to do one thing slowly, without feeling rushed.

Day 69: Powerful Purpose

Scripture:

"For we are God's handiwork, created in Christ Jesus to do good works."

— *Ephesians 2:10 (NIV)*

* * *

Affirmation:

I am walking with purpose that is consistent with my healing and love.

Reflection Prompt:

What purpose or passion has been placed on your heart during this season of healing? What action will you take to get closer to it?

Journal Space:

Reflect & Respond

[69]

---

[69] Consider creating a purpose photo board that shows who you are and what your purpose looks like.

Day 70: Flourish in Faith

Scripture:

"The righteous will flourish like a palm tree, they will grow like a cedar of Lebanon."

— *Psalm 92:12 (NIV)*

* * *

Affirmation:

I am thriving in faith and freedom.

Reflection Prompt:

What helps you trust your growth, even when it's unseen?

Journal Space:

Reflect & Respond

70

---

70 What's one thing you could release emotionally today?

Week 10 Reflection: The Results of Roots

Scripture:

"So then, just as you received Christ Jesus as Lord, continue to live your lives in him, rooted and built up in him, strengthened in the faith as you were taught, and overflowing with thankfulness."

— *Colossians 2:6–7 (NIV)*

* * *

Affirmation:

I am rooted in faith and carrying healing into the way I live each day..

Reflection Prompts:

This week invited you to notice how healing is showing up in your everyday choices.

Faith, awareness, and care are becoming woven into the way you live, move, and respond.

1. Where have you noticed your faith grounding your daily choices more naturally?
2. How has your relationship with your body changed as trust has grown?
3. Which routines or rhythms now support your well-being without effort or resistance?
4. How do gratitude and awareness show up differently than they did before?

Reflect & Respond

Day 71: Flow in Faith

Scripture:

"Trust in the Lord with all your heart and lean not on your own understanding."

— *Proverbs 3:5 (NIV)*

* * *

Affirmation:

I am flowing in the divine flow, trusting in timing and truth.

Reflection Prompt:

Where in your life do you feel encouraged to flow rather than stall?

Journal Space:

Reflect & Respond

[71]

---

[71] Flow into your day. Try taking a deep breath before responding to stress today.

Day 72: Healing Relationships

Scripture:

"Be kind and compassionate to one another, forgiving each other, just as in Christ God forgave you."

— *Ephesians 4:32 (NIV)*

* * *

Affirmation:

I am willing to heal through compassion and honest connection.

Reflection Prompt:

Which connection, past or present, requires peace, kindness, or release for your recovery to progress?

Journal Space:

Reflect & Respond

[72]

---

[72] Forgiving begins with self.

Day 73: Strength in Spirit

Scripture:

"I can do all this through him who gives me strength."

— *Philippians 4:13 (NIV)*

* * *

Affirmation:

I am strong in spirit, steady in purpose, and filled with divine strength.

Reflection Prompt:

How does it feel to have strength come back to your body or spirit?

Journal Space:

Reflect & Respond

---

73 Take time to appreciate your strength. You are doing the work.

Day 74: Living Aligned

Scripture:

"The integrity of the upright guides them."

— *Proverbs 11:3 (NIV)*

* * *

Affirmation:

I am in harmony with my body, mind, and purpose, living authentically and freely.

Reflection Prompt:

What does life in full alignment look like for you right now?

Journal Space:

Reflect & Respond

74

---

[74] Get everything done today that you set out to do, without interruptions or unanticipated consequences.

Day 75: Overflow and Impact

Scripture:

"Freely you have received; freely give."

— *Matthew 10:8 (NIV)*

* * *

Affirmation:

I am growing in excitement and purpose, giving freely from the abundance.

Reflection Prompt:

How might you use your healing or story to help someone else succeed? How can sharing your story help you grow?

Journal Space:

Reflect & Respond

---

[75] Do something special for a loved one.

Day 76: Body Wisdom

Scripture:

"You are altogether beautiful, my darling; there is no flaw in you."

— *Song of Songs 4:7 (NIV)*

* * *

Affirmation:

I am listening to my body's wisdom, which was divinely created to heal.

Reflection Prompt:

What lessons has your body taught you about trust and resilience?

Journal Space:

Reflect & Respond

---

[76] Stop here and listen to the song *"Here I Am to Worship"* by Tim *Hughes.*

Day 77: Joy in the Journey

Scripture:

"This is the day that the Lord has made; let us rejoice and be glad in it."

— Psalm 118:24 (NIV)

* * *

Affirmation:

I choose to rejoice in the process, not simply the outcome.

Reflection Prompt:

How can you bring greater joy into your daily activities?

Journal Space:

Reflect & Respond

⁷⁷

Week 11 Reflection: Walking in Discernment

Scripture:

"Teach us to number our days, that we may gain a heart of wisdom."

— Psalms 90:12 *(NIV)*

* * *

Affirmation:

I am walking forward with wisdom, awareness, and trust in what my body and spirit have learned.

Reflection Prompts:

This week, be mindful to the wisdom that has quietly blossomed inside you. You don't question or chase healing anymore. It has changed how you listen, make choices, and respond.

Take a few minutes to reflect:

1. What wisdom has emerged through this season of healing and renewal?
2. How do you recognize when your body or spirit need adjustment or care?
3. Where do you feel more confident saying "yes" and more peaceful saying "no"?
4. How can discernment guide you into your next season of life?

Reflect & Respond

Day 78: Faith in Action

Scripture:

"For we live by faith, not by sight."

— *2 Corinthians 5:7 (NIV)*

* * *

Affirmation:

I am taking courageous, faithful action in line with my purpose.

Reflection Prompt:

What steps, big or small, can you take today to show your restored faith?

Journal Space:

Reflect & Respond

---

[78] Sit in complete silence for a moment and notice your thoughts
(thoughts are things).

Day 79: Whole-Body Gratitude

Scripture:

"I will give thanks to you, Lord, with all my heart."

— *Psalm 9:1 (NIV)*

* * *

Affirmation:

I am grateful for all aspects of myself—mind, body, and spirit.

Reflection Prompt:

How can you thank your body for everything it has endured and overcome?

Journal Space:

Reflect & Respond

[79]

---

[79] Nourish your whole body with whole foods today.

Day 80: Fruit of Healing

Scripture:

"You will know them by their fruit."

— *Matthew 7:16 (NIV)*

* * *

Affirmation:

I am experiencing the benefits of healing, peace, clarity, and compassion.

Reflection Prompt:

What healing fruits have begun to appear in your life?

Journal Space:

Reflect & Respond

⁸⁰

---

[80] Try a gentle hip stretch to release tension (let go of what's been holding on to you).

Day 81: Harmony Within

Scripture:

"Let the peace of Christ rule in your hearts."

— *Colossians 3:15 (NIV)*

* * *

Affirmation:

I am at peace with myself—mind, body, and soul.

Reflection Prompt:

Where in your life do you currently experience inner harmony, and how can you protect it?

Journal Space:

Reflect & Respond

81

---

[81] Slow down while eating; savor this moment, no rushing. You're winning.

Day 82: Courage to Continue

Scripture:

"Be strong and courageous...for the Lord your God will be with you wherever you go."

—*Joshua 1:9 (NIV)*

* * *

Affirmation:

I am courageous and supported as I continue my growth.

Reflection Prompt:

What does courage mean for you in this next season of healing?

Journal Space:

Reflect & Respond

[82]

---

82 Try taking one step closer to "becoming."

Day 83: Living Abundantly

Scripture:

"I came that they may have life and have it abundantly."

—*John 10:10 (NIV)*

* * *

Affirmation:

I live abundantly in health, joy, and purpose.

Reflection Prompt:

How can you make more room for abundance in your body and your life?

Journal Space:

Reflect & Respond

[83]

---

[83] Fill your cup, so you can give it away. Invite someone to church this week.

Day 84: Faithful Alignment

Scripture:

"Commit to the Lord whatever you do, and he will establish your plans."

— *Proverbs 16:3 (NIV)*

* * *

Affirmation:

I am aligned with divine guidance in every decision I make.

Reflection Prompt:

What does it feel like when your choices align with your values and faith?

Journal Space:

Reflect & Respond

---

[84] Try opening your hands, palms up, and whispering, "I'm letting go."

Week 12 Reflection: Living Whole

Scripture:

"You will go out in joy and be led forth in peace."

— *Isaiah 55:12 (NIV)*

* * *

Affirmation:

I live wholeheartedly, walking in joy and serenity.

Reflection Prompts:

This final week offers space to reflect on the journey as a whole.

You are invited to honor how far you've come and to carry this rhythm of healing forward with intention and trust.

1. How has your life changed since day one?
2. Which therapeutic fruit are you most proud of cultivating?
3. How has this method changed your connection to faith or flow?
4. What truth or rhythm will you carry forward beyond this journal?

Reflect & Respond

Day 85: Renewed Vision

Scripture:

"Where there is no vision, the people perish."

— *Proverbs 29:18 (NIV)*

* * *

Affirmation:

I can see my life clearly through the lens of healing and hope.

Reflection Prompt:

What image of the future resonates with you the most right now?

Journal Space:

Reflect & Respond

[85]

---

[85] Tell someone of your vision...keep going, spread the news!

Day 86: Beauty in Becoming

Scripture:

"May the favor of the Lord our God rest on us; establish the work of our hands."

— *Psalm 90:17 (NIV)*

* * *

Affirmation:

I am embracing the beauty that is unfolding at each stage of my personal growth.

Reflection Prompt:

How has this practice helped you become more compassionate and whole to yourself and others?

Journal Space:

Reflect & Respond

[86]

---

[86] Refresh yourself from the outside in—give yourself a spa day! You've earned it.

Day 87: Sustained Peace

Scripture:

"The Lord bless you and keep you; the Lord make his face shine on you and be gracious to you."

— *Numbers 6:24–25 (NIV)*

* * *

Affirmation:

I am nourished by a peace that sustains through all seasons.

Reflection Prompt:

What practices help you stay calm even in difficult situations?

Journal Space:

Reflect & Respond

[87]

---

[87] Commit to one habit that will help you sustain peace each day.

Day 88: Embodied Faith

Scripture:

"Let us not love with words or speech but with actions and in truth."

— *1 John 3:18 (NIV)*

* * *

Affirmation:

I am living in faith through action, care, and love.

Reflection Prompt:

In what practical way can you show your faith or appreciation today? How did you show your appreciation last week?

Journal Space:

Reflect & Respond

⁸⁸

Day 89: Shine from Within

Scripture:

"Let your light shine before others, that they may see your good deeds and glorify your Father in heaven."

— *Matthew 5:16 (NIV)*

* * *

Affirmation:

I am shining my inner light with confidence and humility.

Reflection Prompt:

How can you spread your healing light into the lives of others?

Journal Space:

Reflect & Respond

[89]

---

[89] Celebrate your dedication and commitment to your faith and healing journey.

Day 90: Rooted and Radiant

Scripture:

"The Lord blesses his people with peace."

— *Psalm 29:11 (NIV)*

* * *

Affirmation:

I am rooted in faith, radiant in joy, and renewed in purpose.

Reflection Prompt:

What does it mean for you to live rooted and radiant beyond these ninety days?

Journal Space:

Reflect & Respond

---

[90] Go be incredible. From soil to soul, plant seeds that enrich others, honoring the reflection of your own becoming.

Pause & Pray

Final Reflection: Rooted and Radiant

Scripture:

"In all my prayers for you. I always pray with joy because of your partnership in the gospel from the first day until now, being confident of this, that he who began a good work in you will carry it on to completion until the day of Jesus Christ."

— *Philippians 1:4-6 (NIV)*

* * *

Affirmation:

I honor the work that has been done within me and trust the growth that will continue.

Reflection Prompts:

Over the past ninety days, you have practiced listening, resting, renewing, and growing. Healing has unfolded in layers, sometimes quietly, sometimes with clarity.

This reflection is not about evaluating or perfecting your journey. It is about honoring the effort, faith, and presence you brought to each page.

Take your time here. Let gratitude lead.

1. What moments from this journey feel most meaningful or transformative?
2. How has your relationship with your body changed since the first day?

3. What new rhythms, beliefs, or practices feel rooted in you now?
4. Where do you notice more peace, trust, or self-compassion in your life?
5. How do you want to carry this sense of healing into your days ahead?

Reflect & Respond

Pause & Pray

Conclusion

"He who began a good work in you will carry it on to completion until the day of Christ Jesus."

— Philippians 1:6 (NIV)

* * *

You've spent the last ninety days slowing down, listening to yourself, and planting seeds of healing.

What has changed can be small: a calmer breath, a gentler thinking, or a lighter heart.

You could have just started to sense roots growing below the surface.

They are all holy steps forward.

There is never a straight route to healing. As you practice it, it becomes a living rhythm.

As you move forward, remember what you've learned here: get enough rest, feed your spirit every day, and have faith that growth often happens silently before it blooms.

Let the rhythm of regeneration continue in you—one mindful breath, one faithful step, and one gentle flow at a time.

Afterword

Keep going on your journey.

Healing doesn't stop here; it keeps going as you develop. What you've done over the past ninety days can serve as a lifelong pattern of renewal.

Here are some moderate methods to keep going:

1. Begin again...

Each season we learn something new. You can read this journal again whenever you feel the need to get your mind, body, and spirit back in flow.

2. Talk about the practice.

Ask a friend, family member, or small group to go through these pages with you. Sharing your healing makes it deeper.

3. Keep taking care of your roots.

Stay connected for more tools, reflections, and resources for whole-body renewal.

For new publications, guided reflections, and group resources, go to www.forwardthinkerwellness.com or follow @ForwardThinKerPress.

4. **Be rooted, rested, and rejuvenated.**

Carry this rhythm with you; growth doesn't stop when the pages do. Every thought—like every seed—has the power to grow into lasting healing. Let the ideas you've planted here grow where you need them the most.

May every breath remind you of the rhythm of regeneration, and may peace flow through you, steady and lively, like light moving through the soil of your soul.

Until the next season of growth, keep listening, healing, and blooming.

— Jackie

About the Author

Jackie Frary is a wellness advocate, functional health coach, and author who believes healing begins when we reconnect the mind, body, and spirit.

After years of navigating mystery symptoms and fatigue, Jackie became the CEO of her own healing, integrating functional medicine principles with faith-centered mindfulness, nourishment, and grounded lifestyle practices.

She is the author of *The Internal Fungus Among Us* and founder of Forward ThinKer Wellness and Forward ThinKer Press, where she creates wellness education and resources designed to support restoration, resilience, and purposeful living.

Jackie is certified in Nutrition, Life and Wellness Coaching, Ayurveda, and body-based therapeutic practices, and she is passionate about walking alongside others as they seek wholeness, clarity, and hope.

When she's not writing or collaborating with wellness and faith communities, Jackie can be found hiking, journaling in quiet coffee shops, or teaching others how to listen to the wisdom of their own bodies. Her *From Soil to Soul*™ series continues to grow, with future books centered on **rooted living, inner renewal, and the slow work of restoration**.

www.forwardthinkerwellness.com
Facebook: ForwardThinKerWellness
Instagram: @jackieftwellness

Also by Jackie Frary

The Internal Fungus Among Us—A Functional and Faith-Centered Journey to Heal the Gut-Brain Connection and Renew Your Energy (Forward ThinKer Press, 2025)

Future titles and wellness resources available at *www.forwardthinkerwellness.com.*

www.ingramcontent.com/pod-product-compliance
Lightning Source LLC
Chambersburg PA
CBHW051425130726
47987CB00005B/1921